MEDIEVAL LIVES

Stonemason

ROBERT HULL

A⁺
Smart Apple Media

Smart Apple Media is published by Black Rabbit Books

P.O. Box 3263, Mankato, Minnesota 56002

Printed in the United States

Published by arrangement with the Watts Publishing Group Ltd, London.

Library of Congress Cataloging-in-Publication Data

Hull, Robert, 1935–

    Stonemason / Robert Hull.

    p. cm.—(Smart Apple Media. Medieval lives)

    Summary: "Traces the life of a typical stonemason in medieval times from birth to death, including childhood, training, masonry jobs that were available, and retirement. Includes primary source quotes"— Provided by publisher.

    Includes index.

    ISBN 978-1-59920-173-3

    1. Stonemasonry—History—To 1500—Juvenile literature. 2. Civilization, Medieval—Juvenile literature. 3. Stonemasons—Juvenile literature. 4. Europe—History—476-1492. I. Title.

TH5421.H85 2009

693'.10940902—dc22

2008000445

Artwork: Gillian Clements

Editor: Sarah Ridley

Editor-in-chief: John C. Miles

Designer: Simon Borrough

Art director: Jonathan Hair

Picture research: Diana Morris

Picture credits:

Ark Religion/Alamy: 23, 25b. Asperra Images/Alamy: 17t. Biblioteca Nazionale Marciana Venice / Gianni Dagli Orti /The Art Archive: front cover, 5. Biblioteca Nazionale Turin/Roger-Viollet /Bridgeman Art Library: 28. Bibliothèque de l'Arsenal Paris/Giraudon/Bridgeman Art Library: 36. Bibliothèque des Arts Decoratifs Paris/Archives Charmet/Bridgeman Art Library: 9. Bibliothèque Municipale Castres/Giraudon/Bridgeman Art Library: 12. Bibliothèque Nationale Paris/Alfredo Dagli Orti/The Art Archive: 20. Bibliothèque Nationale Paris/Giraudon/Bridgeman Art Library: 24, 33, 34. Bodleian Library Oxford/The Art Archive: 11. British Library Board/Bridgeman Art Library: 14. Alistair Campbell/UK City Images/Topfoto: 19. Castle Museum Ferrera/Alfredo Dagli Orti/The Art Archive: 26. Paul Felix Photography/Alamy: 21t. Michael Jenner/Alamy: 27. A F Kersting/AKG Images: 30. Paul Maegaert/Bridgeman Art Library: 35. MEPL/Alamy: 22. Florian Monheim/Roman von Götz/Alamy: 8. Musée Condé Chantilly/Giraudon/Bridgeman Art Library: 10, 16. Museo Opera del Duomo Firenze/Bridgeman Art Library: 32. James Osmond/Alamy: 39. Picturepoint/Topham: 13. Private Collection/Bridgeman Art Library: 40. Ray Roberts/Alamy: 41. St Lorenz Nuremburg/Bridgeman Art Library: 38. Jeff Saward/Labyrinthos Photo Library: 37. Spectrum Colour Library/HIP/Topfoto: 18. Staatsbibliothek Nuremburg/AKG Images: 31. Jack Sullivan/Alamy: 29b.

9 8 7 6 5 4 3 2 1

CONTENTS

INTRODUCTION

The medieval period of European history is from approximately 1000 to 1500. It was a period of momentous events. In 1066, England was conquered by the Norman French duke, William, and his men. William was crowned king in December 1066. During most of the fourteenth century, France and England fought a series of wars called the Hundred Years' War. In addition, Christian crusaders fought with Muslim Arab armies over the control of Jerusalem. The Black Death, or plague, in 1348, killed approximately one-third of the population of Europe.

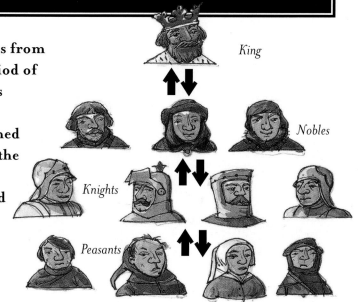

King

Nobles

Knights

Peasants

Feudal Society

At the beginning of this period, European society was feudal. Kings owned all the land, but a class of knights was granted land in return for service in war. Knights made similar arrangements with holders of manorial estates, and they, in turn, with those below them, down to the peasants who were granted a few acres of land. The peasants were "tied" to the land in return for fees and heavy service obligations. This network of agreements held society together.

As time went on, society became less feudally organized. Money payments and rents took the place of services and payments "in kind." As more transactions were made in

Gothic cathedrals such as this one were built throughout the Middle Ages.

Medieval artists often depicted mythical building sites. The Tower of Babel, shown here, was a popular subject.

money, more money came into circulation. There was a rapid development of trade and towns. The population of Europe increased. The ability to buy things with money spread to all groups, except the poorest. The wealthiest people spent freely on buildings in stone, a trend that accelerated when timber began to grow scarce and became expensive.

Building in Stone

A vivid picture of the shift from timber buildings to stone—and one way it was funded—is found in the *Chronicle of Jocelin, Abbot of Brakelond* in Norfolk from 1173:

❖ *At this time too, our almonry was rebuilt in stone—formerly it had been ramshackle and of wood. Walter the physician, then almoner, gave a large donation of money that he had made from his medical practice.* ❖

The guesthouse was also rebuilt:

❖ *See how on the abbot's orders the court resounds to the sound of pickaxes and stonemasons' tools as the guesthouse is knocked down . . . May God provide for the rebuilding.* ❖

Churches Abound

The French chronicler Ralph Glaber, writing in the eleventh century, wrote about the boom in church building:

❖ *It is as though the very world had shaken herself and cast off her old age, to clothe herself everywhere in a white robe of churches.* ❖

Building Explosion

The early medieval period in particular—from about 1000 to 1250—was an astonishing time for constructing ecclesiastical buildings in stone. Cathedrals, abbeys, nunneries, and monasteries were built of stone. Numerous outbuildings sprang up in or near large towns or in the countryside. Stone churches replaced timber churches in thousands of villages. In France, there was a church for every 200 inhabitants.

It was not only the church that funded stone buildings. Kings and some noblemen did too. Numerous castles, colleges, and even manor houses of stone appeared. Each one needed an army of stonemasons to quarry stone, cut and carve it, then lift and lay it in place.

Many of these stone buildings, some glorious, some modest and plain, survive today. This is the story of the typical life of a stonemason who worked on these buildings.

BIRTH

In an upstairs room in a fairly large house compared to most in the town, the stonemason's wife is about to give birth. The town's midwife and two women neighbors are present. No men can enter the room.

To ensure a safe and easy delivery, the stonemason's wife has asked for a scroll to be laid across her belly during childbirth. It has a cross on it that is one-fifteenth the size of the cross on which Jesus was crucified. As her time draws close, the women pray to the saints and urge the mother to do well. The child—a boy—is born safely. The scroll and the prayers seem to have worked.

Urgent Baptism

A fourteenth-century poem by Robert Mannyng grimly stresses the urgency of early baptism.

❖ *Adam's sin was so severe*
That there is none to God so dear
Who will not to hell be gone
Unless he is washed in the font of stone. ❖

Baptism

The parents want the boy baptized as soon as the godparents—two godfathers and a godmother—can come to the church and give him a name.

Carrying his Latin manual, or book of services, the priest meets the midwife, baby, and godparents on the church porch. He asks the sex of the baby. A boy—so he is placed to the priest's right. Before entering the church, the priest frees the boy from inherited evil by exorcising him. The priest performs various gestures, makes signs of the cross over the boy's forehead, and asks his name.

The priest puts a little salt in the baby's mouth. Then he spits in his left hand and uses the thumb of his right to moisten the boy's ears and nostrils with saliva—the way Christ healed a deaf mute. After two or three more signings of the cross, the party goes into the church to the font.

A baby being baptized at the stone font.

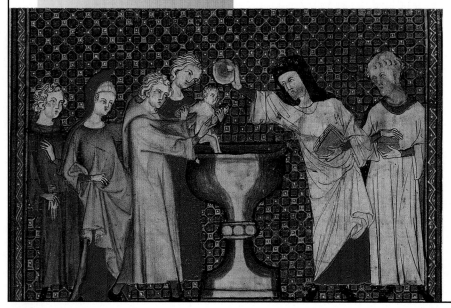

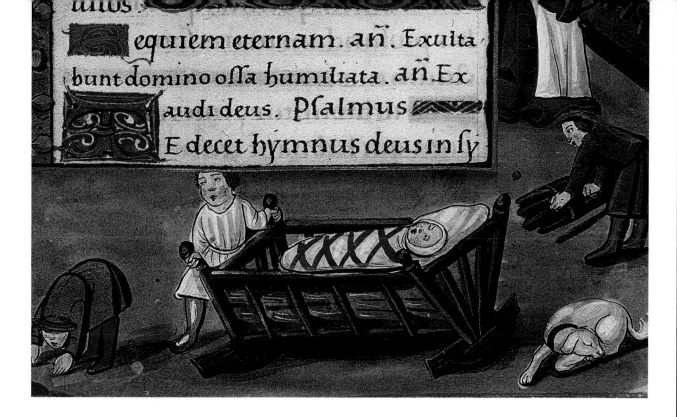

equiem eternam. añ. Exulta
bunt domino ossa humiliata. añ Ex
audi deus. Psalmus
E decet hymnus deus in sy

Three full immersions take place in the water of the font. The baby is then wrapped in a blessed robe. The godparents are told to teach the child simple prayers. The parents (though the mother is not present) are to keep him safe.

The mason gives a small feast for family, neighbors, friends, and godparents in the evening. They bring the baby boy gifts—a small toy or a little money.

The Churching

The mother cannot go to church to give thanks for having safely given birth. She is not allowed to touch a holy object or enter a holy place for 40 days because, having given birth, she is considered unclean. Only when she is "churched," purified in a ceremony at the church where

she goes with women neighbors and friends, can she resume her normal life.

Though the stonemason and his wife are, like most people, Christians, they put food by the baby's cradle at night. This is to appease any wicked spirit or witch who might want to harm their child.

The little boy soon crawls. He learns to walk with the help of a wooden frame and then on his own. He is carefully watched in case he wanders near the fire or bowls of boiling water. There are dangers in the street with horse-drawn carts as well as roaming cattle and pigs that have escaped from their pens. He survives these dangers and is growing up strong and healthy.

A baby wrapped in swaddling bands in its cradle, which is on rockers, is being rocked by an older child.

Exorcising Sin

The church believes that every baby inherits the "original sin" committed by Adam and Eve. At the baptism, an exorcism is performed for the baby to renounce his sin. The priest asks the baby simple questions in Latin. The godparents reply on his behalf.

❖ *Abrenuncias Sathane? (Do you renounce Satan?)*
Abrenuncio. (I renounce him.)
Quid petis? (What do you seek?)
Baptismum. (Baptism.) ❖
After that, all is well.

CHILDHOOD AND GROWING UP

Even the healthiest children get sick. When he is four, the stonemason's son becomes ill, as do many children in the town. His mother is desperately worried. She measures the length of his small body and has her husband buy a candle of exactly the same length to take to the church as an offering. Her son recovers—the cures have worked.

Home Schooling

At the age of five, the boy's mother starts to teach him his letters. She buys biscuits, sugary fruit, and cakes in the shape of letters. His father gives him a primer with the alphabet and buys educational toys, such as the small windowed box that shows one letter at a time as a little wheel turns around the scroll inside. He also carves small stone animals for his son and buys metal soldiers and a mechanical bird.

School

The parents want their son to learn. The father is keen for his son to become a stonemason, perhaps a master, who might one day build a cathedral. At seven, his son goes to a school in the church. A priest teaches reading and writing, Latin grammar, and arithmetic. The boy will need to know Latin to read the many documents and papers of the time.

Boys being taught to read by a priest.

12

Childhood Games

When he is not at school, there are games to play in the street. He might spin a top, run along on a stick horse, play with little windmills on sticks, or roll stones. Sometimes, there are fairs to go to and feast days to celebrate.

By the time he is nine or ten, the boy occasionally goes with his father to the quarry or the building site. He watches stones being hewed, shaped, and carried and the mortar being mixed. At the site, his father gives him a chisel and hammer to carve on a piece of spoiled stone.

.Confabulator.

Confabulatio. īa. ē vīa cīp ſompni. Electo ⁊ueiens ſic uoleis vozmīr. iuiam. velectībȝ i melioratī et vigoiiet ⁊ſenſi ⁊ ſpū. ſigcumūm anoir ples ⁊fabulatozes. cū uoluit ñ unū. auō Regiō noctī ipoueit ſei enmi. illi q̄ anoir nō eiſ. Couueit oibȝ ⁊ploubȝ oibȝ etatibȝ. pter puis. oī tp̄: ſi mag breme.⁊ regioi bitute.

Children and parents gathered around the fire.

Drawing

The father gives his son simple drawings to do using compasses and a square that he uses when planning a building. The young boy plays with circles, half-circles, intersecting circles, circles in squares, and straight lines ending in arcs—the basic shapes for designing buildings. He feels he is working like a real mason. At 13, he has already decided to be a stonemason and work alongside his father.

TRAINING AT THE QUARRY

T he teenage boy begins work with his father, who is the master mason for a new church a short distance from their town. The boy will help where he can, learning as he goes. At 15, he is old enough—and strong enough—to do some work as his father's assistant and be trained by him.

Health and Safety

His first "schoolroom" is the quarry. The mason warns his son about the dangers of quarries and building sites and reminds him to keep his wits about him. Stones, wood, heavy tools—and men sometimes—fall from scaffolding; platforms collapse; blocks of stone fall off carts. During the previous week, a mason's legs were broken by a fully loaded cart.

Woodmen cut down trees and masons rough dress blocks of stone.

Although there were attempts to regulate the wages on building sites, they were probably determined as soon as the master or under master was in a position to judge the mason's level of skill. In October 1304, at Caernarvon Castle, 53 masons received 17 different rates of pay. In October 1316, there were 24 masons on 12 different wage rates. The presence of servants and apprentices at different stages in their training may have contributed to this variety of pay scales. In some cases, there were also women laborers.

Learning His Trade

The son learns from his father about building with stone. Stone that is suitable for castles, town walls, or pavements is usually not right for shaping or intricate carving. That is why this quarry has been chosen, even though the hills between the quarry and the church will add to the cost of transportation. Transportation usually increases the price of quarried stone by about four times, unless it can be taken by water some of the way, which it can here. It also keeps weight and cartage costs down if some stones are carved before they leave the quarry. Sometimes cities plunder their own walls to build cheaper churches.

The father takes his son to see a skilled quarryman at work at a new rock face. First, he estimates how wide the layer of stone is and where it is best to start cutting. He uses a pickaxe, crowbar, and wooden wedges. He makes the backbreaking work look easy.

Stone dust is everywhere in the air. The boy watches laborers with a crane and claw lifting stones into wheelbarrows—a recent invention—and carrying them to waiting carts.

The Mason's Mark

His father gives the boy his mark. He will put his mark on every stone he cuts. A master mason must know who carved every stone—even in a huge cathedral. Any stone that is the wrong size or shape, out of line, or hollowed instead of flat, results in the responsible mason losing pay.

The boy's main training work now is to scapple hewn stones. This means shaping them roughly (rough dressing) with an axe and a hammer. The stones are then ready for carting down to the river and on to the building site.

The son helps his father with some of the rough dressing of stones at the quarry.

TRAINING AT THE BUILDING SITE

As master mason, the boy's father can make sure his son experiences all the different tasks on the building site so he will begin to understand the work of masons.

With several laborers, the boy carries water, lime, and sand to the man mixing mortar. He watches the man work, then carries the mortar in a tub on his back. He walks quickly as the mortar will start to set. He enters the church and walks to the screen being built with beautifully carved stones.

Later, he helps the setters to put intricate moldings and tracery into windows and arches. He helps the men lay stone blocks in place—sometimes he is high up on the scaffolding.

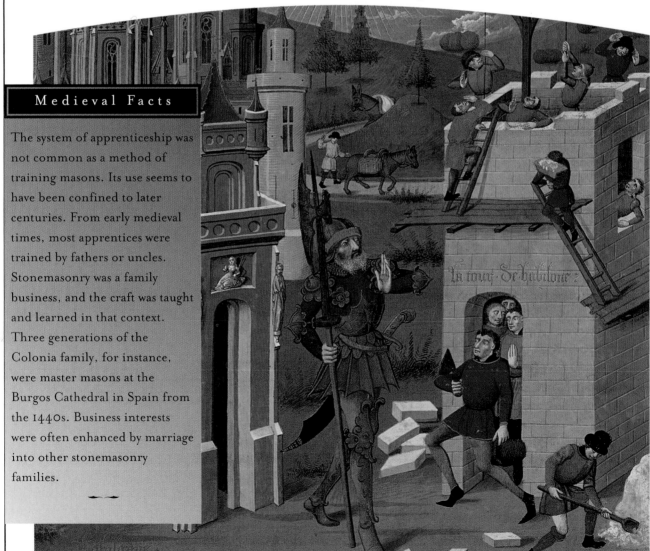

Medieval Facts

The system of apprenticeship was not common as a method of training masons. Its use seems to have been confined to later centuries. From early medieval times, most apprentices were trained by fathers or uncles. Stonemasonry was a family business, and the craft was taught and learned in that context. Three generations of the Colonia family, for instance, were master masons at the Burgos Cathedral in Spain from the 1440s. Business interests were often enhanced by marriage into other stonemasonry families.

Dressing Stone

His father sets him to work as a cutter, shaping rough-dressed blocks to the exact sizes that are needed. He must keep the edges straight, the curves correctly curved, the corners at a right angle, and the surfaces flat. It is difficult to get this all right. After months of dressing all kinds of stones, destined for different parts of the church, he is given drawings of one or two small detailed shapes to carve on bits of spare stone: an oak leaf and an ox. This is even more difficult, but the boy finds the work fascinating.

His training is going well. He learns quickly how to use the set square and compasses. He learns to use a variety of other tools. These include a variety of chisels to create smooth surfaces and a large cone-shaped mallet of applewood for delicate work. For months, he works on decorating blocks with moldings—designs carved onto the stone with the help of a template—a thin layer of wood that has the exact shape needed.

To the Tracing Floor

The father is very pleased with his son's progress. Now he takes the son to the workshop to transfer his scale drawings on parchment to life size by using a tracing floor of plaster. This floor is brushed clean for each drawing, leaving ghostly outlines underneath as examples for the stone to be carved on. One or two life-size designs are even engraved on the stone floor of the church, ready for copying.

His son watches, then practices the same skills with two or three designs his father needs for window openings high in the church. He also works on designs from buildings he has drawn. Then he spends many months on the freehand carving of objects he has observed or drawn—oak leaves, an apple, a gate, piglets, and human faces.

The father watches his son develop over several years. His son seems skillful enough to do well as a stonemason.

A mason's mark chiseled on a stone block.

WORKING AS A ROUGH MASON

The young man is ready to set out on his own. If it were not for the fact that his father, who has become prosperous, wants to spend more time on the other trades he and his wife have begun to build up, the young man would have remained working with him. Now his father prefers to run an inn and tend grazing animals. But also, his lungs have been affected by inhaling stone dust over so many years.

On His Own

This does not deter the young man from his chosen vocation. He hears that masons are needed for repair work on a damaged bridge in the nearby town. The upkeep of the bridge is the responsibility of the wardens of the bridge. However, funds come from the surrounding towns and villages whose travelers and traders use it. One group of villages looks after a pier and a cutwater, another group pays for the upkeep of the roadway.

He presents himself to the master mason in charge of the bridge works. He tells him what he has learned over the last few years— from cutting and carrying stone to carving in freestone from templates and drawing up designs.

He is taken on as a rough mason at not much above the laborer's rate and is paid by the hour. He has to rough dress blocks of stone and

make them ready for the skilled cutters to shape exactly—work he knows he can do just as well. He must cut into the stone his mason's mark and the sign that indicates where it will go on the bridge. He is warned that every block is checked by the master mason, and any faults will mean loss of up to two days' pay.

This medieval stone bridge at Cahors, in central France, still stands.

This mural tower in Canterbury would have been built by masons working for the town. The clock is modern.

has more work to do in the town. He needs to construct a short tunnel and build walls of stone as firebreaks between thatched timber houses. He asks if the young man would like to join him on those projects.

The answer is yes. After working on both projects, the young mason gains more experience and earns a growing reputation for being hardworking and trustworthy. He learns more about the geometry of construction and feels that his mason's career is now properly launched.

Perhaps he can afford to marry the young woman worker he met on the first building site. His father promises him that when he marries he will give him a small house in the town.

First Success

His first work goes well. The master mason is pleased with him and gives him the work he wants, which is to dress stones exactly to make them ready for laying in place. The master mason trusts him to go to the quarry to choose more stone. When the bridge repairs are finished, he says that he

SUMMONED TO WORK AT A CASTLE

The young man's first work away from home is about 50 miles (80 km) away. He has been impressed—summoned— by the king to work on the stonework of the main hall in one of his new castles. It takes him over two days to walk to the castle carrying his compasses and set square. The hammers, chisels, other tools, and protective gloves are to be provided by his employer.

The Working Day

The under mason explains that his working day will be from sunrise—before 5:00 A.M. in summer—to sunset. He will work five-and-a-half days a week, finishing at noon on Saturday. He has one hour for dinner, 30 minutes for resting, and 30 minutes for a break in the afternoon. He will be paid for feast days and days of travel, though not when bad weather stops work. If his work is not up to standard (uncunning), he can be dismissed. That would be done before noon. The work will last for several weeks.

Because he is inexperienced, he is to work as a rough mason, at the summer rate of 4 pence a day, rough dressing stones. With his training and some experience, he feels he will be accepted everywhere soon as a real mason, but he has to prove himself here. The stones he rough dresses must be right. Otherwise he will not only lose pay, he will lose the under mason's confidence. Once he gains it, though, he might be given stone to finish properly or even carve designs.

Laborers and masons at work on a castle; the overseer is on his horse.

A collection of the stonemason's many tools and some templates.

Medieval Facts

Impressment by the monarch might even threaten to take masons from their work on large and important projects. In 1441, All Souls College in Oxford obtained a royal order to exempt men working there from being impressed by the king to work on Eton College.

The stonemason with his basket of tools.

To Work

He gets his tools—chisels, hammer, stone axe, and wooden mallet—from the lodge, the shed-like structure built against the walls. He will do some of his work here and have his midday rest—until the bell clangs to start work. His living and sleeping quarters are in a hostel that the employers have built nearby.

It is the young man's first experience on a large building site. The constant noise surprises him at first. From early morning until nightfall, the air rings with the squeal of pulleys and windlasses; the sounds of hammers, chisels, saws, and axes; and voices shouting orders and warnings. It sounds chaotic, but it is not. The site is highly organized.

The under mason soon sees the quality of the young man's work. He is given more responsibility and now turns the rough-dressed stones into precise sizes and shapes. The under mason promotes him to the rank of mason. His wages are increased from 4 pence to 6 pence a day.

The mason and the young woman decide to marry. In a year or so, his father will give him the small house he promised.

The young man has earned the right to be called a mason. That is a beginning, but his father says there are many ranks of mason on most big building sites. It will take time and hard work to become one of the better-paid masons and even longer to fulfill his dream to become a master mason and design a cathedral.

That is the future. His next step now, he believes, must be to work on a large church. A new abbey church is to be built approximately 20 miles (32 km) from his home, which is still his parents' house when he is not away working. He will walk home to see his wife whenever he can.

A mason cuts a piece of stone to size with a frame saw.

To the Abbey Church

With compass and square, the young mason sets off for the abbey. He heads for the lodge, a one-story wooden structure built against a wall of the small, old church. Damaged in a storm, the old church is being demolished. A grander building—the abbey church—will replace it.

In the lodge, there is a space for laying out and tracing drawings and a work area for making the wooden templates that help to produce exact replicas of carved work. Tools are also stored, sharpened, and repaired here. Stones are cut, dressed, and carved here too. The master mason is often in the lodge discussing work with other masons or hiring labor.

First Skilled Carving

The young mason tells him about his work, his training, and experience. The master mason takes him on as a journeyman mason, paid by the day. He is given work to do dressing stones. The master mason is soon convinced by the young mason's abilities and asks him to do a trial carving of a mouse on one side of some spoiled stone. The young man tackles this with enthusiasm. It is his first chance since his training to show how well he can carve freestone—stone which can easily be shaped on all its faces (or sides) and sculpted into patterns or lifelike representations of foliage, animals, human faces, and so on.

He carves the mouse to the master's satisfaction and is given the task of first dressing the curved stones of a doorway arch. Then he will carve the chevron shapes that give a pleasing patterned effect to the archway.

In time, he is asked to try other shapes too. He enjoys sculpting grotesque faces like those he has seen on other buildings. He completes one of a man with a toothache that becomes one of the abbey church's gargoyles. He knows his new son will like it when he is old enough.

Medieval Facts

The word "sculptor" seems to have been seldom used in medieval times, except in Italy. There were artist-craftsmen all over Europe doing work that we would call wonderful sculpture. But they were thought of as cutters or carvers of stone—although highly skilled and experienced—rather than masons in a special category. Nonetheless, the reputations of the most skilled cutters and carvers traveled far. Perhaps this is why sometimes, experienced as they were in all kinds of stonemasonry, they readily became under masons or master masons.

The young mason spends two years dressing stone and carving designs on the abbey church. In winter, when building stops because of the frosts, he continues to work on his carving and on drawing geometrical designs.

Work Stops

The flow of money and bequests has temporarily stopped because the king has embarked on a war. The abbey has to sell precious objects and divert spare funds to pay taxes to finance this war. The mason has more opportunities now to walk the 20 miles (32 km) home to his wife and son in their small new house.

In the meantime, by different routes, from rumor to recommendation, the young mason's skill and capacity for hard work and his artistic talent with hammer, chisel, and mallet become known to other potential employers. With two other masons, he is rewarded by being presented—a considerable honor—with gifts of winter clothing.

The Image Carver

When work starts again, the bishop tours the new building with the master mason. The bishop asks the young mason if he will work as an "imaginator" (image maker) in

A working drawing for part of the great cathedral in Laon, France, showing the ox heads that decorate the pinnacles.

smaller churches being built or rebuilt in his diocese. The young mason would carve delicate

In 1414, the authorities of Valencia Cathedral engaged in preparations for a new bell tower. A contract was drawn up to pay their architect to research bell tower structures in other cities.

❖ *It is settled that Pedro Balaquer, an "able architect," shall receive 50 florins from the fabric fund of the new campanile (bell tower) . . . in payment of expenses on the journey he made to Laredo, Narbonne, and other cities, in order to see them and examine their towers and campaniles, so as to discover from them the most elegant and suitable form for the Cathedral of Valencia.* ❖

Finding Inspiration

Before he begins to carve a single piece, the bishop wants him to travel to other churches and cathedrals—even one or two in another country. The bishop asks the mason to see what kinds of decorative works are done in other churches and collect ideas. He wants the young man to take inspiration from the work of the best stone artists. The bishop expects the images in his churches to be up-to-date and as interesting as possible.

On his travels, the young mason sees sculptures he had never encountered or imagined. He sees oxen sculpted on high pinnacles in honor of the animals who draw carts. He makes sketch after sketch, and by the time he returns, his drawing book and his mind are full of ideas.

stonework and lead three or four other sculptors. He would choose what to work on and how to treat it.

The young mason wonders if his ambition to be a master builder will be helped or held back by working, perhaps for several years,

as a carver of images. He finally decides that if he builds a reputation as a mason who can execute the highest quality images, construct memorable and moving designs, and lead others, it will help him rise further in his craft.

This statue of the Virgin and Child is in Reims, France.

Rewards, usually in money or clothing, were sometimes paid to masons for good work. An entry in the Eton College accounts from 1445-46 states:

❖ *In various rewards made to setters of stone . . . for their diligent labor in hot weather . . . Henry Roo 12s . . . and to five . . . setters of freestone, 5s 8d, 6s 4d, 2s 8d, 3s 4d, 3s 4d; but then to a carver 20s.* ❖

STONE CARVER

The master mason tells the stone carvers about the kind of images the bishop hopes to see in his churches. He would like figures from a religious story over each west door. In each nave, he wants a strong image of the church's patron saint. But he leaves their imaginations free to work on things such as capitals, gargoyles, and panels.

Our carver visits the churches, all three within miles of each other. He decides to work first on two capitals for a nave, the space where the village people gather. He will carve the capitals on-site in the large church's lodge.

Gathering Ideas

He discusses with the other carvers what they will do. In their lodge at the largest church, they spend time drawing sketches for possible designs. They exchange ideas and compare drawings. The carver's notebook reminds him of vivid images he has seen. These include a tombstone with a panel showing scholars listening intently to a lecture; a full-size sculpture of a woman lying down and reading a book; a grim facade depicting the torments of hell; and relief carvings of a Bible story. There were many more, including some hideous devils.

He decides first on a homely, slightly comical scene with a hint of sin in it—a boy stealing fruit from an orchard. It will please the ordinary worshippers, as well as—

he hopes—the master mason and their patron. As he begins carving, another idea comes to him. When he has time, he will draw it.

This twelfth-century carving of a boy picking fruit is in the cathedral in Ferrara, Italy.

Medieval Facts

Some of the finest carvings in medieval churches and cathedrals were done in pure white marble, some in the polished Purbeck or Corfe marble that was really a compressed limestone. Many carvings, from the fifteenth century on, were done in polished white alabaster. Chellaston in Derbyshire was known for its high-grade alabaster. In 1414, Alexander de Berneville, a master mason working for the Abbey of Fécamp, France, traveled to Chellaston to buy alabaster. He paid 40 gold crowns for it to be shipped to France through Hull.

Carving Images

Work gets underway at the large church. The carver's first capital is eventually ready. He marks it with his mark and a number indicating where it will be placed. He likes it, as does the master. The painter will give color to the face on the capital, so it will gaze down even more intently into the nave.

He starts work on his second, more complicated idea: Saint Matthew writing as he receives inspiration from an angel who bends down to him. However, one of the sculptors nearly spoils his angel by carving the foot and giving it a sandal. Of the main religious figures, only the Virgin Mary, a human being, has shoes—not God, nor Jesus, nor the angels. Luckily, it is not too late. The carver is skilled enough to chisel away the sandal down to the bare foot hiding in the stone, before anyone notices. This too proves successful.

His work is approved, and the master gives him a new panel to work on—one he can fill with a design of his own. He decides on a favorite story, the creation of the animals.

An effigy of a noble and his wife rest on their tomb in Spilsby, Lincolnshire. Nobles liked to be commemorated by sculptures such as these.

THE LODGE

The skilled stone carver has spent much of his time in the lodge at the largest church working alongside other masons. In various ways, he has learned to appreciate the lodge. It gives him shelter from bad weather. He can take blunt or damaged chisels and axes to the blacksmith to have them sharpened or repaired on the spot. He finds, too, that as trust builds up between different masons, ideas, notebooks, and drawings are shared and knowledge is exchanged. The lodge becomes as much a living community as a building of wood.

The Emperor Charlemagne founds the abbey at Aix-la-Chapelle in this manuscript illustration that also depicts masons at work and cranes lifting blocks of stone.

Lodges

Lodges were clearly work places and at first only that. At Beaumaris Castle in 1330, timber was bought to repair:

❖ *a tumbledown house . . . in which the masons ought to work.* ❖

At Vale Royal Abbey, Cheshire, in 1278 to 1280, six barrow men were paid for carting stones:

❖ *. . . to be cut at the masons' lodge.* ❖

Sharing Experiences

It is helpful to hear stories of the others' travels to buildings elsewhere in the country and in other countries. It thrills him to learn about wonderful buildings, amazing high spires, and a spire that is not solid but a frame of stone you can see through. He hears of buttresses that "fly" to walls and statues on the highest pinnacles of the roof.

He hears about towers that fall because they were built too high on columns that were not solid. He learns of walls that lean, crack, and bulge because the foundations were shallow, filled with the wrong material, or the mortar was not mixed properly.

Code of Conduct

Two carvers know of attempts to get all masons in the country to agree on and write rules for their craft. This would include a rule that an apprentice's training take five to seven years. Other rules would be that masons should not take another mason's work or give away the secrets of their trade—such as constructing designs from geometric shapes—to a non-mason. The masons should also take communion once a year.

The carver believes these are things a good mason practices anyway. However, it would be good to have these written down and agreed on, perhaps throughout the country. It would show patrons that masons take their work seriously and consider being a mason an honor. Masons are not of high social standing because they work with their hands. But the skilled carving mason is an artist. The master mason is a leader, engineer, and a designer who works with a set square and compasses to make designs for great buildings. Their work needs more recognition and status.

Members of the lodge with tools and symbols of their craft.

Symbols and masons' tools decorate this stained-glass window of a modern Freemason's lodge.

The mason soon takes another step upward. His highly skilled work as a carver of images has often been praised by the bishop. He is asked to take on the job of under mason, sometimes called warden or parleur, in the building of a college. He will be the person to explain the master mason's ideas and ensure that masons understand the plans. He also has to keep a watchful eye on building materials, tools, and equipment that can mysteriously disappear.

The Under Mason

As deputy to the master mason, he will help appoint new masons. He will have responsibility for some of the designs and drawings. So not only will he visit the quarry and be on hand all over the building site, he will spend a good deal of time in the lodge workshop checking on the work of other masons, working out designs and doing drawings on parchment, and making designs on the tracing floor.

Meanwhile, masons come to the site looking for work. He asks them to do trial work on spoiled stones or stones put to one side outside the lodge. He checks to see what tools they have brought with them. The building works usually supply and repair the cheaper tools, such as axes, hatchets, hammers, and chisels. But masons are expected to bring their own set square and compasses with them, simply because they are too expensive to provide.

Theft

At York Minster in 1345, the Fabric Roll shows that there were worries about loss of materials through theft:

❖ *Item, be it noted that, as regards the church fabric, he (the Keeper of Fabric) says that alienation of timber, stone, and lime has often occurred, and he does not know where . . . he says that more evils arise from the quarry and at home nothing suitable for the fabric is carried away.* ❖

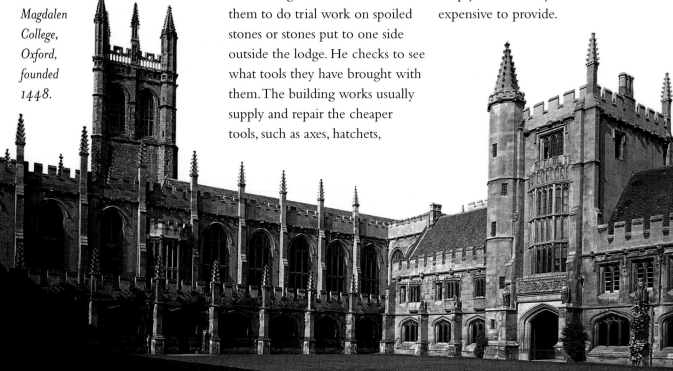

Magdalen College, Oxford, founded 1448.

This fifteenth-century German painting shows a skilled roofer at work in Nuremburg.

Site Manager

With the master carpenter, he supervises the building of a second lodge. The old lodge provides working space for about 20 masons, but more masons are being taken on as the college grows. More tools are being bought and will need to be stored. There are also a few training or apprentice masons working with older masons, mainly family members. Space has to be found for them as well.

The college is out in the country, 30 miles (50 km) or so from his home. The under mason also ensures that workers are accommodated properly in the hostel—a simple wood structure—specially constructed for them.

These are time-consuming responsibilities and take him away from his beloved stone, mallet, and chisels. However, he is learning quickly about the complicated organization of a building site.

MASTER MASON FOR THE CATHEDRAL

More than 100 miles (160 km) away, a new cathedral is to be built. Four well-known masons have been asked to travel there to meet the money-providing patron—the bishop—and the chapter. Each mason will describe what his plans would be if appointed to the position of master mason.

To the Interview

The mason makes the long journey on foot. The bishop and chapter give him some idea of what they want. An important consideration is size. The city's population is increasing. The cathedral must be high enough, long enough, and impressive enough. It must be both beautiful and modern in spirit to be worthy of a great city and, of course, hold a large number of people.

The skilled mason carver and imaginator, with fresh experience as an under mason, is one of those summoned. He has thought long and often about the cathedral he would like to build. He brings his notebook with a hundred drawings of his ideas and one or two models in wood.

This model of the cupola atop the Duomo in Florence was the work of a brilliant architect, Filippo Brunelleschi (1377-1446).

The mason shows his drawings and plans. He brings a model and clearly explains what he would do. The patron understands the model better than the complicated drawings. He and the chapter like the model and the mason's clear, dynamic way of speaking. They appoint him. His young wife is thrilled, even though it means they will have to move.

32

Appointed as Master Mason

The master will direct a large number of craftsmen. Carpenters and joiners will construct pulpits, choirs, pews, and a screen. Blacksmiths will make hinges, locks, nails, and railings. The glaziers will produce windows and colored images. Plumbers will put down lead sheeting on the roof. The painters will paint wall scenes and images.

He will select many of the craftsmen. But he will have an under master or warden to help him. A clerk of the works will handle all the business details, including wages. His own wage will be about four times what

Another view of the construction of the cathedral at Aix-la-Chapelle.

he earned as an image carver. He will be allowed to claim his travel expenses.

The bishop and chapter are pleased that he is more than willing to take on all of this responsibility. Before they meet again, he is asked to prepare more designs and drawings, so they understand even better what he plans to do.

DESIGNING THE CATHEDRAL

The site of the new cathedral has been selected by the bishop and his chapter. The money is provided by the bishop. Work will begin at the east end, the most sacred space. This is where the high altar will be and where the relics will be kept. The cathedral will be positioned so that the east windows light up at sunrise on the birthday of the cathedral's saint. As soon as possible, the east end will be roofed and consecrated, so that pilgrims can visit.

Completing the Plans

These things were decided before the master mason begins his work. Now he needs to complete his plans. He translates his sketches into detailed scale drawings of the nave, arches, chancel, altar, and side chapels. He also works on plans for the triforium and clerestory. He wants the vaulted roof and spire to be the highest in the region.

He is ambitious to design a beautiful cathedral that will have higher and wider pointed arches than other cathedrals he has seen. There will be less heavy stonework and more glass and light. He travels to other cathedrals and building sites to see how other masters have solved their problems.

This plan of the tower of Laon Cathedral also shows a bearded head and a Gothic window.

34

The cloister, or covered quadrangle walk, of Gloucester Cathedral (built 1370-1410) boasts a fan-vaulted ceiling.

Too many walls, spires, and towers fall down for him to take any chances with his design. A high tower or spire always puts great stress on the columns beneath, around the crossing in the middle of the building. The high pointed vaults he wants to build also set up stress and can push the walls outward where they come down onto the columns. He studies one cathedral where the walls are braced against this outward push by "flying" buttresses that he has heard about. These are not built against the wall as part of it, but stand separately.

Lime Pits and Quarry

He also has to make sure that lime pits—to make lime mortar—are dug months in advance of the start of building. More importantly, he decides which of three nearby quarries to use. With the bishop, he visits all three and decides he would like to use the furthest away of the three. The extra distance will increase carting expenses, but it has the honey-colored sandstone he wants for "his" cathedral. The bishop agrees. However, the marble and the alabaster for the intricate carving will be found elsewhere.

He is now ready to set in motion the actual building of the cathedral.

BUILDING THE CATHEDRAL

The master's first task is to supervise the pegging out on the ground, with ropes, the dimensions of the cathedral. The blacksmith makes him a square-sectioned length of iron, approximately 16 feet (4.8 m) long. This pole will measure out all of the cathedral's main dimensions—vertical and horizontal.

Down the length of the cathedral, the distance between one column and the next is one pole, as is the distance between each column and the outer walls. The side aisles are a pole wide, while the nave is two. This makes the structure four poles wide. The length from east to west will be twelve poles. Its height will be a breathtaking six poles.

Final Preparations

Next, the master has the foundations dug and filled with rubble to make them solid. The foundations have to be deep. If they are shallow—or the infill is not sturdy enough—sinking or cracking occurs; walls can lean and even collapse.

Medieval Facts

In laying out the design for a cathedral, the basis of the measurement was a large unit of length or module. This length might vary from country to country and even region to region, but it did not vary within the building site. Spaces and lengths were planned and measured in terms of this modular length. This helped to give buildings their balance and proportionality.

The master mason and his patron check on the progress of the building and inspect the work of masons, carpenters, and mortarers.

He redraws his scale designs life-size on the tracing shop's plaster floor. He recalls with gratitude his father's training and the years tracing scale drawings, making templates, brushing the surface clear, and starting another drawing. This is the true source of his cathedral—its curves and arches and vaults, its repeated shapes and decorative graces.

He meets many craftsmen, with a view to employing them. He decides on a master carpenter and a master smith. He interviews several stonemasons. He employs most of them but at different rates of pay depending on their skill.

Building Starts

The work is underway. With templates, masons can work to the right shapes and sizes. Precision is essential: raising a massive stone to the top of the wall and finding it does not fit wastes time and money. The walls and their scaffolding are rising quickly.

The stones are wheeled from carts into the lodge. They are shaped and carved, ready to be positioned. All day long, weighty stones are lifted and swung high in the air by cranes with grappling hooks run by worker-powered treadmills and wound up by windlasses. Carpenters have learned to build lifting gear to handle very heavy stones. This eliminates the need for a great deal of scaffolding. The master's young son comes with

him sometimes and watches it all with fascination. He loves drawing too, just as his father did at the same age.

The master watches everything with satisfaction. He knows that if he is able to work here for a few years, he will see a cathedral begin to rise over the city. This will show the bishop and chapter that appointing him was the right decision. The city will see that a beautiful cathedral will be theirs in time. To accomplish his dream, he works from dawn to dusk; his wife hardly sees him.

A view inside Chartres Cathedral, France, shows the famous labyrinth (maze) on the floor of the nave.

Words of Caution

❖ *An honorable work glorifies its master, if it stands up.* ❖

These wise words of caution were written by Lorenze Lechler, a German master mason, in his "Instructions" booklet on design that he put together for his son in 1516.

FULFILLMENT AND RETIREMENT

The master works for 10 years on the cathedral. It has risen high into the air, almost to its roofline, higher than he had expected to see it. It is many years from completion, but still a magnificent sight visible from miles away on the roads into the city.

He is now 50 and beginning to wish that he had the energy he once had. He proudly envies his son, an accomplished stone carver already. A younger man would find it easier to spend the day endlessly climbing stairs and ladders to check on the progress of the work.

Leaving the Cathedral

It is the right time to leave—for the cathedral and for him. His work over the last 20 years has made him very prosperous; he can now afford to bring his career as a stonemason to an end. He wishes to do one last carving—an image of himself as master mason contemplating the model that he showed the bishop and chapter 11 years ago.

The bishop and chapter agree to this request. They greatly value all he has done. One of their rewards is to assure him that his designs and plans will be followed by any master mason who succeeds him. Another— jokingly—is to promise they will not order him out of retirement, whatever difficulties the cathedral may have in the future.

They also wish to have a tombstone for him in the cathedral when he eventually dies. He knows this is an honor, and he gratefully accepts.

Adam Kraft, the fifteenth-century master mason of Saint Lorenz, Nuremberg, sculpted a self-portrait with his mallet in hand.

Some people could not stop building. The fourteenth-century Italian merchant, Datini, had what the Italians called *la malattia del calcinaccio* — "rubble disease." A friend's letter is full of concern that while his house is being built he spends entire days:

❖ *. . . among masons, workmen, mortar, sand, stones, cries and despair. . . . No cart is filled without your lending a hand, no stone or brick laid without your changing its place, with a lot of shouting and general carrying on.* ❖

The solid central tower of the cathedral in Wells, Somerset, soars above the surrounding countryside.

At the end of medieval times, a new interest developed in the classical world and the harmony of its buildings. In particular, it contrasted with the dominant medieval style that began to be called Gothic architecture. Classical architecture was refined and harmonious; Gothic was considered crude and backward. New buildings were designed by a new type of architect-scholar whose experience and ideas were not derived from work experience on building sites but essentially from books and theories. This type of "architect" began to replace the master mason. In the 1570s, Phillip II of Spain employed Juan de Herrera—a man with no practical experience in building or design—as the official architect.

Final Projects

He leaves the cathedral, but his days as master mason are not over. There is one more project. He wants to build a farmhouse just outside of town where he has kept sheep and cattle. He will live a more settled and quiet life among fields, animals, and orchards. He throws himself into this work—mainly a timber building. He hires carpenters, tillers, and brick layers. But he keeps the building and design under his control.

In a year or so, the house is almost finished. Soon he spends much of his time farming his small estate with his wife at his side. The rest of his time is spent making a start on his final building—a house for his son.

END OF A LIFE

Though, at the age of 60, the mason thinks of death, he does not brood over it. He feels lucky to feel well. He remembers mason friends who, like his father, have died not being able to breathe—their lungs choked with stone dust. He thinks of all the men he has seen over the years, and women laborers too, who have fallen or been pushed from scaffolding or roofs. Others have been crushed by carts or toppling stones or killed by falling stones. He even knows of one master mason who was murdered. He has survived many years of dangerous work.

A memorial slab over the grave of a seventeenth-century stonemason. It would be a great honor for the mason to be commemorated in this way.

His Achievements

He is proud of what he has achieved, especially some of his memorable carvings. Other masons now travel to admire and make sketches of these. They also visit the new cathedral that he regularly goes to see. Work has begun on the spire—his spire, for true to their promise, the bishop and chapter have kept scrupulously to his original designs.

The mason finally falls ill from one of the great waves of sickness that passes over the land every few years. He dies within days, without taking Extreme Unction—the final anointing by the priest before death with a final confession of sins. Like many people, he believed that would only make death more likely.

Funeral Mass

The Statutes of Regensberg, Switzerland, stipulate that if a master builder dies while he is working on a building site:
❖ *A mass must be said for the soul of the deceased. All the masters and workers should be present and should make a small financial contribution.* ❖

Medieval Facts

When he died in 1263, Hugues Libergier, master builder of Saint Nicaise in Reims, France, was accorded the honor of a tombstone in the church. His engraved figure, as befitting a person of status, stands under an arch wearing a hat, a long robe, and a hooded cloak. He holds a model of the church and a measuring rod. At his feet are a set square and a pair of dividers—the other essential tools of his profession. Clearly, he was a socially important figure.

Commemoration of His Work

His grief-stricken wife, son, and family friends watch over his body at the wake. Later, mass is sung for him and attended by all the stonemasons working on the cathedral, as well as many other workers. He is buried within the cathedral.

The church pays for his funeral and arranges for a mass to be sung every year for the master's soul. A tombstone is begun with a carving of the master mason, complete with robe, set square, and compass. It will be done by his successor, the master mason who now hopes to build much of the rest of the cathedral.

In his will, the master mason leaves all his tools and books of drawings to his son, except for the drawings done for the cathedral. He leaves those to the cathedral lodge. He bequeathes money to maintain and train two apprentices. His best work will remain for hundreds of years in the standing structure of the cathedral.

This fine statue in Dijon, France, depicts Claud Suter, the master mason who built the ducal palace there.

GLOSSARY

Alabaster ❖ a stone especially suitable for carving statues

Almonry ❖ a place from which alms were distributed

Apprentice ❖ someone undergoing formal training for a set period—rough mason apprenticeships might last only three years, others five or seven years

Bishop ❖ the head of a diocese—elected by the chapter or appointed by the pope or the king

Buttress ❖ a mass of stone or brick built against a wall to give it strength

Capital ❖ the top of a column

Chancel ❖ the east end of a church or cathedral where the altar is

Chapter ❖ the governing body of a church or cathedral, led or presided over by the bishop

Choir ❖ the part of the chancel where the religious officials stood and sat to perform the offices

Crypt ❖ the burial place under the church or cathedral

Diocese ❖ a district under the control of a bishop

Dress ❖ to dress stone is to carve it to size

Fabric Roll ❖ the record of costs and payments on everything from wages to the purchase of stone; called a roll because the parchment it was written on was rolled up

Feudalism ❖ the system of holding land in return for agreed services, works, or payment in kind

Flying buttress ❖ a structure standing separate from the wall it buttresses and "flying" up to it, providing extra support for the roof

Freemason ❖ a word used in later medieval times for the mason who carved stone

Freestone ❖ stone suitable for carving

Gargoyle ❖ or gurgle hole—a carving, sometimes grotesque, on a stone rainwater spout

Gothic ❖ a style of architecture prevalent in Europe from the twelfth to sixteenth centuries, characterized by pointed arches

Imaginator ❖ a carver of images, a sculptor

Impressment ❖ conscription or summons by the king or the church to work on a building project

Lodge ❖ a simple covered wooden structure built against the wall of a building where work was done and tools kept; later on, also a body of masons working there

Manor ❖ a feudal estate held by a lord with its own manor court

Mason ❖ a worker in stone

Mass ❖ the central religious service of the medieval church, enacting the ceremonial consumption of bread and wine, the body and blood of Christ; sung by the priest in Latin

Master mason ❖ mason in charge of all the craftsmen and workers on a site and often the designer (architect in modern terms) of a building

Money ❖ pounds (£), shillings, and pennies, or pence were the main coins used in Britain in medieval times; a mark was a coin worth 13 shillings 4 pence

Nobles ❖ high-ranking people such as lords or archbishops; also a coin

Patron ❖ someone who contributed funds to start up and support building projects

Pounds ❖ *see* Money

Priest ❖ the clerk in charge of the church; sometimes a rector or vicar

Primer ❖ a small handwritten manuscript with extracts for children to learn how to read

Payment in kind ❖ payment with articles of produce, such as eggs

Relief ❖ carving shapes onto stone so they stand out

Rough dress ❖ a first stage in shaping stone roughly to size

Rough mason ❖ a mason who only roughly shaped stone before it was handed to a carver, cutter, or freemason to shape precisely

Scapple ❖ to rough dress stone

Screen ❖ a stone or wood structure separating the nave of a church from the choir and chancel

Shillings ❖ *see* Money

Stone cutter or cutter ❖ a stonemason who carved stone to precise shapes and sizes

Template ❖ a frame or piece of wood (or zinc in later times) shaped exactly to the desired size and dimensions of stones to be carved

Tracery ❖ thin ribs of stonework

Tracing floor ❖ the area where full-scale drawings of parts of a building were incised in plaster

Under mason ❖ deputy or second-in-command to the master mason

Wake ❖ the ceremony of watching, overnight, the dead person's body

Windlass ❖ a wooden structure for winding up weights with pulleys

TIME LINE

Note to parents and teachers:

Every effort has been made by the publishers to ensure that the Web sites in this book are suitable for children, that they are of the highest educational value, and that they contain no inappropriate or offensive material. However, because of the nature of the Internet, it is impossible to guarantee that the contents of these sites will not be altered. We strongly advise that Internet access be supervised by a responsible adult.

ca. 910 on	Feudalism is established.
1065	Dedication of Westminster Abbey.
1066	William of Normandy invades England and is crowned king in December.
1085	Domesday Book survey.
1093	Durham Cathedral is begun.
1096	Norwich Cathedral is begun.
1096	The First Crusade begins.
1098	Cistercian Order is founded.
ca. 1100 on	Powerful religious revival in the twelfth and thirteenth centuries.
1107	Winchester Cathedral falls.
1110 on	Anglo-Norman churches have carved chevron pattern in England.
1137	Work starts on Abbey of Saint Denis, Paris.
1162	Thomas Becket is consecrated as Archbishop of Canterbury.
1163	Cathedral of Notre Dame is begun in Paris.
1170	Becket is murdered by knights who believe it was what King Henry wanted.
1174	King Henry does penance for the murder of Becket.
1174	Fire at Canterbury Cathedral—rebuilding starts.
1194	Another fire at Canterbury Cathedral—rebuilding begins.
1207	The Order of Saint Francis is formed in Italy.
1208	King John quarrels with the pope who bans church services in England.
1209	Magdeburg Cathedral is begun.
1214	Barons demand charter of liberties from King John.
1216	Saint Dominic's order of friars (traveling preachers) is approved by the pope.
1218	Salisbury Cathedral is being rebuilt in Gothic style.
1220	Work begins on Amiens Cathedral.
1222	Work begins on the Burgos and Toledo cathedrals.
1260	The design for Strasbourg Cathedral is drawn up.
1260	Chartres Cathedral is consecrated in Chartres, France.
1277	Work starts on castles in North Wales for King Edward I.
1305	Clement V becomes the pope; the papacy move to Avignon.
1337–1453	Hundred Years' War between France and England.
1348–1349	The bubonic plague (Black Death) spreads through Europe.
1361	Europe experiences another outbreak of the plague.
1377	Avignon "captivity" of papacy ends.
1389	First translation of the Bible into English.
1414–1418	End of Great Papal Schism.
1440	King Henry VI founds Eton College.
1449–1471	Colonia family are master masons at Burgos and Vallodolid cathedrals.
1450	Invention of printing with moveable type.
1450–1471	Wars of the Roses.
1460s	First medieval books on architecture begin to be published.
1490	King Edward IV's youngest daughter enters a nunnery.
1530s	Monasteries and nunneries are dissolved with the Reformation.

INDEX

These are the lists of contents for each title in *Medieval Lives*: